CONTENTS

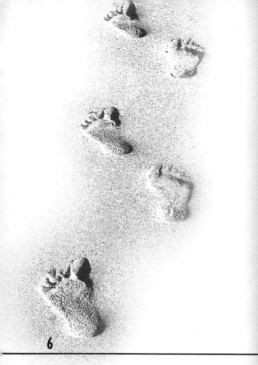

Introduction

HOW TO USE THIS BOOK

This book is designed to help you lead others through a basic study of the Christian faith. *A Follower's Life* includes twelve sessions and covers three major areas of study: Life in Christ, Life in the Spirit, and Life in Community.

Naturally, the sessions are designed to be taught in twelve consecutive weeks of study. However, because the units are largely self-contained, you can restructure the course in various ways, depending on the specific needs of your church.

For example, many churches prefer to offer one course for "basic Christianity" and another for "church membership." *A Follower's Life* makes that adaptation easy—since the first eight sessions deal with our personal relationship with God, while the last four sessions focus on our responsibility to worship and serve within a local body of believers. By splitting the course into two parts, you can address the needs of those who simply want to investigate the Christian faith without pressure as well as those who are ready to consider making a more serious commitment to your local church body.

If you restructure the course in this way, however, we suggest that you make the first course (Sessions 1-8) a prerequisite for the second (Sessions 9-12). That way you can be confident that those who wish to officially join your congregation will already have a basic understanding of their own faith.

The sessions are designed to be easy to follow and prepare. Each session provides a list of supplies that you will need and step-by-step instructions for both activities and discussion. Handouts are included at the end of each session and can be photocopied for

A FOLLOWER'S
Life

12 GROUP STUDIES

ON WHAT IT MEANS

TO WALK WITH JESUS

Flagship church resources

from Group Publishing

Innovations From Leading Churches

Flagship Church Resources are your shortcut to innovative and effective leadership ideas. You'll find ideas for every area of church leadership including pastoral ministry, adult ministry, youth ministry, and children's ministry.

Flagship Church Resources are created by the leaders of thriving, dynamic, and trend-setting churches around the country. These nationally recognized teaching churches host regional leadership conferences and are respected by other pastors and church leaders because their approaches to ministry are so effective. These flagship church resources reveal the proven ideas, programs, and principles that these churches have put into practice.

Flagship Church Resources currently available:

- *Doing Life With God*
- *Doing Life With God 2*
- *The Visual Edge:*
  Compelling Video Connectors for Your Worship Experience
- *Mission-Driven Worship:*
  Helping Your Changing Church Celebrate God
- *An Unstoppable Force:*
  Daring to Become the Church God Had in Mind
- *A Follower's Life:*
  12 Group Studies on What It Means to Walk With Jesus
- *Leadership Essentials for Children's Ministry*
- *Keeping Your Head Above Water:*
  Refreshing Insights for Church Leadership
- *Seeing Beyond Church Walls:*
  Action Plans for Touching Your Community
- *unLearning Church:*
  Just When You Thought You Had Leadership All Figured Out!

With more to follow!

A Follower's *Life*

12 GROUP STUDIES

ON WHAT IT MEANS

TO WALK WITH JESUS

Carolyn Slaughter
&
Sherry Douglas

Flagship church resources
from Group Publishing

Group's R.E.A.L. Guarantee to you:

Every Group resource incorporates our R.E.A.L. approach to ministry—a unique philosophy that results in long-term retention and life transformation. It's ministry that's:

This is EARL. He's R.E.A.L. mixed-up. (Get it?)

Relational
Because student-to-student interaction enhances learning and builds Christian friendships.

Experiential
Because what students experience sticks with them up to 9 times longer than what they simply hear or read.

Applicable
Because the aim of Christian education is to be both hearers and doers of the Word.

Learner-based
Because students learn more and retain it longer when the process is designed according to how they learn best.

A FOLLOWER'S LIFE

Visit our Web site: **www.grouppublishing.com**

CREDITS
Editor: Michael D. Warden
Senior Editor: Paul Woods
Chief Creative Officer: Joani Schultz
Copy Editor: Lyndsay E. Bierce
Book Designer: Jean Bruns
Photography: EyeWire
Computer Graphic Artist: Joyce Douglas
Cover Art Director: Jeff A. Storm
Cover Designer: Alan Furst, Inc.
Production Manager: Peggy Naylor

ISBN 0-7644-2346-0

10 9 8 7 6 5 4 3 2 1   11 10 09 08 07 06 05 04 03 02

Printed in the United States of America.

your students' use.

As background on what it means to be a follower of Jesus, you might want to encourage your class members to be reading *Spiritual Entrepreneurs* or *Real Followers*, both by Michael Slaughter, as you proceed through this study.

A Note About Leaders: Class leaders are critical, not only to the quality and success of this course, but also to the relationship of participants with the church. Class leaders are often among the first points of church contact for the participants. Therefore, the leaders must have a deep understanding of the Christian faith and your local congregation.

We encourage co-leadership based on the fundamental principles of discipleship and the example of Jesus sending out disciples in groups of two. Leadership could consist of co-teachers or a teacher and an apprentice (someone who is being discipled to teach). The teachers must

- believe that God has called them to this ministry;
- have spiritual gifts in the areas of teaching and/or exhortation;
- have the quality of life appropriate for a leader or role model;
- be sensitive to people; and
- be willing and able to spend the time necessary to get ready for each class through prayer, study, and preparation.

In addition to the regular sessions, we encourage you to organize for your participants at least two fellowship events outside the regular class setting. This will help assimilate newcomers into the community life of your church. One of these fellowship events should include your senior pastor, allowing your participants to personally meet your pastor and to ask any questions they may have about the church or the Christian faith.

SECTION *1*

LIFE IN CHRIST

Who Is Jesus? (Part 1)

SESSION 1

BEFORE THE SESSION

Make one photocopy of the "Who Are You?" handout (p. 17) and the "What Is the Bible?" handout (p. 18) for each person.

OPENER:
Who Are You?

Once everyone has arrived, have participants form groups of four to six. Give each person a pen and a copy of the "Who Are You?" handout (p. 17). Say:

> **Using the information sheet I've provided, take a few minutes to get to know one another in your small group. Share your names, families, occupations, hometowns, and how long you've been coming to the church. In addition, share one fact about yourself that no one in your group knows.**

After up to twenty minutes, have each group merge with another group. Then ask participants to take turns introducing their own group members to the members of the other group. When everyone has finished, gather participants and collect the handouts.

Open your session with prayer, asking God's Spirit to guide the

SUPPLIES NEEDED:

- Bibles
- "Who Are You?" handouts (p. 17)
- "What Is the Bible?" handouts (p. 18)
- newsprint
- tape
- markers
- paper
- pens

class as participants work together to learn the truth about God, the church, and the world. After the prayer, say:

> *A Follower's Life* **is a survey course designed to give you an overview of Christianity. In the first eight weeks, we will cover two basic areas: Life in Christ and Life in the Spirit. In the final four weeks of this course, we will cover Life in Community. Since this course is foundational to understanding what it means to be a Christian and to have a personal relationship with Christ, we encourage you to make a commitment to attend all the sessions. If for some reason you cannot attend all the sessions, please talk to me after the class to see if we can work out a way for you to participate fully.**

(Note: If you have participants who cannot attend all the sessions, you might consider tape-recording or videotaping those sessions that they will miss. Or you might prefer to set up a separate one-on-one session to cover the material that the participants would otherwise miss.)

Say:

> **We'll begin our survey of Christianity by exploring the most foundational question that everyone must answer: Who is Jesus?**

BIBLE EXPLORATION:
Who Is Jesus?

Tape a sheet of newsprint to the wall, and ask participants to call out definitions or descriptions of how various people define Jesus. For example, participants might say Jesus is called "a great teacher" or "a good man" or "a prophet like Mohammed." Use a marker to write participants' responses on the newsprint. Ask:

- **How do most people come to these sorts of conclusions about Jesus?**
- **How do they know whether or not they are right? Explain.**

Pull out one of the "Who Are You?" handouts from the previous activity, and ask the person whose handout it is to come to the front of the room. Pass around the handout, and ask various people to tell the class something about that person based upon what's written on the handout. After a minute or so, thank the person, and have him or her sit down. Then ask:

- **On what are you basing your conclusions about this person?**
- **How is that different from the conclusions about Jesus that we've listed on the newsprint?**

Say:

People have many opinions about who Jesus is, but not many of them are based on any sort of authoritative source. The sad truth is that many ideas about who Jesus is are nothing more than baseless opinions. So how can we know who Jesus really is? We're going to go to the most authoritative source we know of—one that will give us the facts about who Jesus is. I'm talking about the Bible.

Read aloud 2 Timothy 3:16. Then give each person a copy of the "What Is the Bible?" handout (p. 18), and go over the information together. Be sure to answer any questions that participants may have about the origins of the Bible or its reliability as an authoritative source of information and instruction.

Say:

The Bible has so much to say about who Jesus is that we cannot cover all the information in one session. Therefore, in this session we will focus mainly on what the first part of the Bible, the Old Testament, has to say about Jesus. There are over three hundred references to the person called the Messiah in the Old Testament. As we explore the Old Testament together, we will look at key prophecies that give specific insights about the coming Messiah and then look in the New Testament to see whether those prophecies were fulfilled in Jesus.

God gave us all these prophecies for a purpose. Let's turn to Isaiah 48:3-5 to discover that purpose.

13

Have a volunteer read aloud the passage. Then say:

Clearly, God wanted his people to know who was in control of all that was being done. No credit was to go to gods of wood and bronze. Foretelling Jesus' purpose and seeing the fulfillment in his life authenticated Jesus as God's plan for humankind. Let's take some time now to examine some of these prophecies and see what they tell us about who Jesus is.

Form six groups, and give each group paper and pens. It's OK if a group is just one person. Assign each group one of the following Scriptures:

- Group 1—Isaiah 7:14; Matthew 1:18-25
- Group 2—Micah 5:2; Matthew 2:1
- Group 3—Isaiah 40:3; Matthew 3:1-3
- Group 4—Isaiah 35:4-6; Matthew 9:32-35; 11:2-6
- Group 5—Zechariah 9:9; Luke 19:29-36
- Group 6—Isaiah 53:12; Luke 23:34; 2 Corinthians 5:21

In their groups, have participants discuss the Scriptures assigned to them. Challenge them to look for the Old Testament prophecy and the New Testament fulfillment of that prophecy. Have them write their observations on the paper you've provided. Tell them to be prepared to share their findings with the rest of the class.

When groups are ready, have them share what they've discovered. For your convenience, here is a list of the major prophecies each group explored:

- Group 1—A virgin would have a child who is the divine seed of the Holy Spirit.
- Group 2—The Messiah would be born in Bethlehem. He is before all things and has always existed from eternity.
- Group 3—The Messiah would be preceded by a messenger— that is, John the Baptist.
- Group 4—The eyes and ears of people would be opened; many miracles and healings would be performed.
- Group 5—The King would arrive on a donkey.
- Group 6—The Messiah would bear the sins of many and intercede for those separated from God.

After every group has shared, say:

These are only a few of the hundreds of references or prophecies of Christ found in the Old Testament, but they give us an understanding of God's perfect plan. And they help us begin to understand the amazing truth about who Jesus is.

BIBLE APPLICATION:
Who Do You Say That I Am?

Say:

The question "Who is Jesus?" is one that everyone must answer at some point in his or her life. Jesus even asked his own disciples that very question while he was still in human form on earth. The incident is recorded in Matthew 16:13-19. Let's look there to see how his disciples responded to this very important question.

Ask a volunteer to read the passage aloud. Afterward, give a slip of paper and a pen to each person. Say:

Jesus asked his disciples, "Who do you say that I am?" I'd like for you to answer that question right now. Based on all we've learned so far about Jesus, who do you say Jesus is? Please write your response to that question on the slip of paper I've given to you. You do not need to put your name on the paper. I will collect the papers when you have finished.

When everyone has finished, collect the papers. Ask class members to sit quietly and close their eyes as you read aloud their responses to the question "Who do you say that I am?" After reading all the responses, pray for the class, asking God to reveal to them through his Word the truth about Jesus and themselves.

15

TAKING ACTION:
Life Change

After the prayer, have participants form pairs. Have partners tell each other one or two ways in which their lives have changed or they hope their lives *will* change as a result of learning the truth about who Jesus is.

When pairs have finished, dismiss the class. As people leave, remind them to do the homework provided at the end of the "What Is the Bible?" handout (p. 18).

Who Are You?

Name: _____

Address: _____

Phone: _____

Birthday: _____

Marital Status: _____

Children's Names & Ages: _____

Occupation: _____

What do you do for fun?

What's special about you that you want people to know?

How long have you attended this church?

What do you hope to gain from this class?

How would you describe what it means to be a Christian?

How would you describe your faith experience up to this point in your life?

WHAT IS THE BIBLE?

The Bible is God's means of communication with us in written form. It consists of sixty-six books, but one story is told through the entire Bible. It is the love story of a personal, holy God who created human beings to be in relationship with himself. When that relationship was broken, this loving God pursued humans and put together a plan to restore their broken relationship. Written over a 1,600-year period by approximately fifty different human authors, this one consistent theme flows through the entire text from Genesis to Revelation: what God was willing to do to be in relationship with us.

Although consisting of one story, the Bible is divided into two sections. The Old Testament is made up of the first thirty-nine books and covers the ancient time period from Creation to around 400 B.C. There was then a four-hundred-year period of silence during which God did not speak through the written Word. The Old Testament time is known as B.C. (before Christ). After Jesus Christ came, time was reordered and is now dated as A.D. (*anno Domini*, "in the year of our Lord"). The New Testament covers the time from Jesus' birth to approximately A.D. 100.

Homework

If you aren't too familiar with the Bible, spend some time acquainting yourself with it this week. You might want to browse through the first four books of the New Testament: Matthew, Mark, Luke, and John. These are the books that primarily tell the story of Jesus.

Who Is Jesus? (Part 2)

SESSION 2

BEFORE THE SESSION

Talk to your pastor or other church leaders to request any printed information they may have regarding your church's beliefs about baptism. Explain that you would like to distribute this information to your class and invite the class to ask the pastoral staff any questions they may have about the role of baptism in salvation or church membership.

OPENER:
Unique Observations

Say:

> As you recall, last week we learned from Scripture that hundreds of years before Jesus was born, the great prophets of Israel foretold his coming. Today we will continue to find out more about the person of Jesus as we explore what his contemporaries said about him and what Jesus himself had to say about who he is. We will also find evidence of the uniqueness of Jesus. Remember that we are looking at all of this in the context of Matthew 16:15: "Who do you say that I am?" Let's begin by discovering some unique qualities about one another.

SUPPLIES NEEDED:

- Bibles
- "He Said, They Said" handouts (p. 24)
- "Jesus Claims to Be God" handouts (p. 25)
- pens
- newsprint
- tape
- markers

Life IN CHRIST

Form groups of three or four. Have participants discuss these questions within their groups:

- **In one sentence, what would your contemporaries say is unique about you as a person?**
- **In one sentence, in what way do you think you are unique?**

Assign each group one of the following sets of Scriptures. Participants will explore these Scriptures to discover some of the ways Jesus is unique.

- Matthew 1:18-25 (He had a unique birth and genealogy.)
- John 8:28-30; 1 Peter 1:19; Luke 23:41 (He is sinless.)
- Matthew 8:23-27 (He performs miracles.)
- John 20:1-10 (He has power over death.)
- Luke 7:48-50; Acts 10:42-43 (He has authority to forgive sins.)
- John 6:35 (He satisfies spiritual hunger.)

It's OK if more than one group is assigned the same Scriptures or if more than one set of Scriptures is assigned to the same group. As groups are working, tape a sheet of newsprint to the wall, and divide it into three columns. From left to right, title the columns "What Makes Jesus Unique," "What Jesus Said About Himself," and "What Others Said About Jesus." Once groups have read their assigned Scriptures, ask:

- **Based on these Scriptures, how was Jesus unique?**

Write participants' responses in the left column. Then say:

Each of us has qualities that make us unique. But the more we learn about Jesus, the more we see that his unique qualities set him apart from every other person who has ever lived. Let's explore more of the unique things that Jesus' contemporaries said about him as well as the unique things that he said about himself.

BIBLE EXPLORATION:

He Said, They Said

Form two groups, and give each person a copy of the "He Said, They Said" handout (p. 24) and a pen. Have one group work together to complete the first part of the handout, while the other group completes the second part.

When groups have finished, have participants form pairs by each finding a partner from the other group. Then have the partners share with each other what they discovered within their groups.

When pairs have finished, gather everyone, and ask volunteers to call out what they discovered in their groups and pairs. Write each response in the appropriate column of the newsprint. Afterward, ask:

- **What's your reaction to Jesus' claims about himself?**
- **What do you think about the claims other people made about Jesus?**
- **How can we be confident that Jesus' contemporaries weren't lying about what they really saw or thought about Christ?**

Say:

All of these persons who knew or lived with Jesus through the good days and the bad days recognized him as God. You may find yourself wondering if these people were writing from their creative imaginations or perhaps because Jesus was a good friend and they wanted to promote him. Let's look at what two of the disciples had to say about this question.

Have someone read aloud Luke 1:1-4 and 1 John 1:1-3. Then say:

Luke was a physician. We learn from his writings that Luke possessed a scientific mind and was interested in knowing and communicating the facts. He was not a person who let his imagination roam when writing about Jesus. In the same way, John makes it clear that he was not writing out of his imagination but as an eyewitness to the events about which he wrote. These independent reports agree on who Jesus was and what he did.

21

BIBLE APPLICATION:
Evidence That Demands a Verdict

Say:

> Because our goal in our Christian life is to be transformed, not merely informed, we must do something with the information we have been gathering. As we consider the question from Matthew 16, "Who do you say that I am?" we must begin narrowing the responses and make an individual decision concerning Jesus. Jesus equates himself with God, and the testimonies of others agree. Each of us must choose to agree or disagree with them.

Give each person a "Jesus Claims to Be God" handout (p. 25) and a pen. Guide the class in walking through the flowchart on the handout to help participants see their need to make a personal decision concerning who Jesus is. If you wish, you can use this narration as your guide:

> *Evidence That Demands a Verdict* by Josh McDowell explains in detail the choices each of us must consider. Jesus claims to be God. That claim leads us to two alternatives: Either his claims are false or his claims are true. If the claims are false, there are again two alternatives: Either he knew his claims were false or he did not know his claims were false. If he knew his claims were false, then he made a deliberate misrepresentation. This misrepresentation would make him a liar, a hypocrite, and a fool since he willingly died for a known lie. If he did not know his claims were false, he was sincerely deluded, and he was a lunatic.

> However, if Jesus' claims to be God are true, then he is Lord. If he is Lord, each one of us has two alternatives of what to do with that reality: We can either accept or reject Jesus as God and Lord of our own lives. We should also

consider that putting off a decision is really a rejection of Christ for now.

So who do you say Jesus is? Is he a liar, a lunatic, or Lord?

TAKING ACTION:

Have participants form pairs, then ask pairs to discuss these questions:

- **Based on what you now know about Jesus, do you think he really is who he claims to be? Explain.**
- **What qualities or claims of Jesus do you find appealing?**
- **What qualities or claims of Jesus disturb you?**
- **If Jesus were here in this room, would you like to meet him personally and spend time getting to know him? Why or why not?**

After the discussion, close the class time with prayer.

He Said, They Said

PART 1

Answer this question for each of the following verses:

What did Jesus say about himself?

- John 8:58

- John 10:9

- John 10:30, 33-38

- John 13:12-14

- John 14:6-9

- John 17:5

- Mark 14:61-64

PART 2

Answer this question for each of the following verses:

What did Jesus' contemporaries say about him?

- John—John 1:1-14

- Peter—Matthew 16:16

- Martha—John 11:27

- Stephen—Acts 7:59

- Thomas—John 20:26-29

- Paul—Colossians 1:15-20

Life IN CHRIST • SESSION 2: Who Is Jesus? (Part 2)

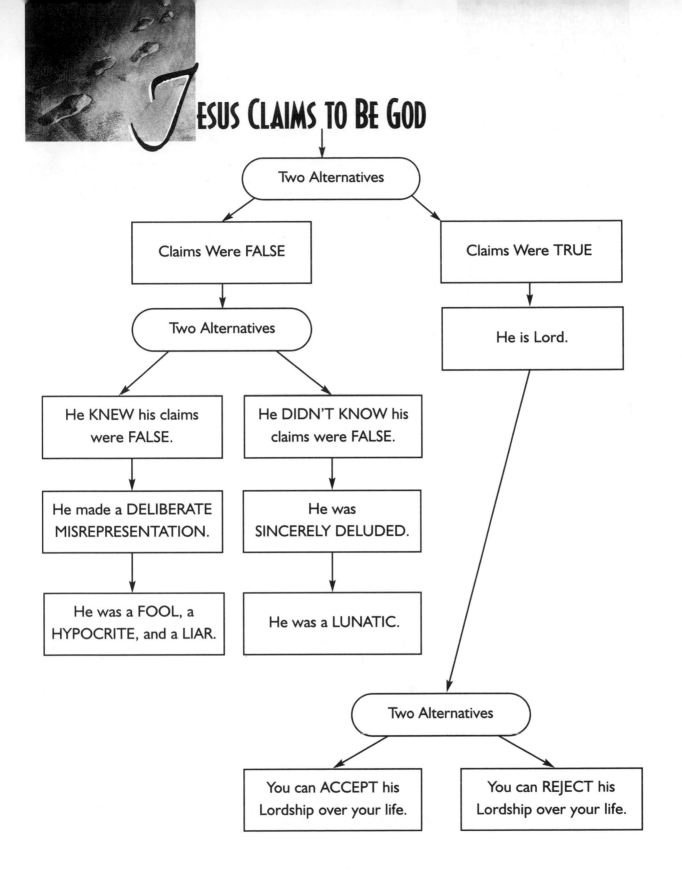

Jesus Claims to Be God

Two Alternatives

Claims Were FALSE

Claims Were TRUE

Two Alternatives

He is Lord.

He KNEW his claims were FALSE.

He DIDN'T KNOW his claims were FALSE.

He made a DELIBERATE MISREPRESENTATION.

He was SINCERELY DELUDED.

He was a FOOL, a HYPOCRITE, and a LIAR.

He was a LUNATIC.

Two Alternatives

You can ACCEPT his Lordship over your life.

You can REJECT his Lordship over your life.

25

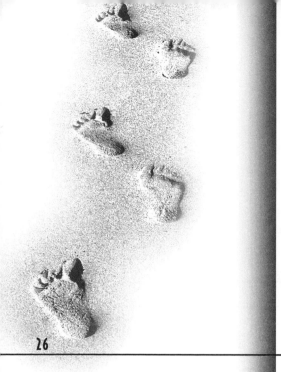

What's a Christian?

SUPPLIES NEEDED:

- Bibles
- "What's a Christian?" handouts (p. 30)
- small gift for each person

BEFORE THE SESSION

Bring to this session a small gift for each class member. It can be as small as a piece of candy. As people arrive, give each person one of the gifts, and tell him or her that it's a little gift from you.

OPENER:

The Bible's Purpose

Begin your session with prayer. Then distribute the "What's a Christian?" handouts (p. 30), and have people form groups of three or four to discuss the following quote from *Spiritual Entrepreneurs* by Michael Slaughter:

"I have visited many Sunday school classes when the people were…studying the lives of Abraham, Moses, David, or one of the other biblical characters. Information is given about 4,000-year-old people, and we feel that the purpose of the class has been accomplished. Scripture was not given for information. It was given that we might see the One who is the author of life and be radically transformed through him."

Ask:

- **How fully do you agree with the message of this statement?**

- **How does the Old Testament help us today?**
- **How does Jesus transform lives?**

After group discussions, have volunteers report the highlights of what they discussed.

BIBLE EXPLORATION:
Why Did Jesus Come?

Have people remain in their small groups from the opener to examine the Scripture passages on their handouts under "Why Jesus Came." Allow people about five minutes on each question. Stop discussion after each section, and have groups report on their discussion. The following is reprinted from the handout for your convenience.

WHY JESUS CAME

For each question below, look up the passages, and discuss the question that follows.

The Sin Problem
1. Isaiah 53:6; Romans 3:10; Romans 3:23; John 3:19
- *What have we humans done to create our own problems?*

2. Isaiah 59:2; Romans 6:23; Romans 14:12
- *What is the result of our actions?*

The Jesus Remedy
3. Isaiah 53:5; Romans 5:8-9; Titus 3:5; Ephesians 2:8-9
- *How did Jesus' coming help us?*

Repentance and Forgiveness
4. Isaiah 55:7; 1 John 1:9; John 1:12; Acts 16:31
- *What must we do to receive salvation in Jesus and enter into a personal relationship with him?*

5. Romans 5:1; Romans 8:1; 2 Corinthians 5:17
- *What does salvation in Jesus mean to us?*

BIBLE APPLICATION:

What Does It Mean to Be a Christian?

Say:

A Christian is someone who has repented of his or her sins, believes in Jesus, has received the gift of eternal life, and has made a faith commitment to Jesus Christ. A Christian's life is grounded in following Jesus daily. We're going to explore three areas of our beings that are involved in that commitment.

Form three groups. Assign each group one of the following areas: Intellect, Emotions, and Will. Have each group discuss the following question as related to the area they've been assigned. Ask:

• **How is one's** [intellect, emotions, or will] **involved in being a Christian?**

Have groups report after their discussions. If the following ideas don't come out in the discussion, you may want to add them.

Intellect

Christianity is based in fact; it is not a *blind* leap of faith. The Gospel writers carefully wrote down the historical record of Jesus' life. Christianity, including the Resurrection, is historical and can be checked out. We are free to investigate everything about our faith, but we must choose to commit to Jesus with our minds.

Emotions

As Christians we enter into a love relationship with the Lord. It is similar to a healthy marriage. In a marriage the couple develops a bond, an attachment that continuously matures the couple's commitment. That bond expresses itself not in feelings alone, but also in loving actions toward each other. We, too, must respond through our actions, demonstrating our love for Jesus. We must love as God first loved us.

Will

When we make a commitment to follow Jesus, it's an act of our will, a choice. To not choose is to choose a life apart from Christ. And living out that commitment is a continuing act of will. If we depend on our emotions and feelings to maintain our relationship, it will falter. Regardless of how we feel at the moment, we are living out of commitment. Once we invite Jesus in, he has promised that he will never leave us or forsake us.

After the reporting, have volunteers read aloud the following passages: 2 Corinthians 5:17; John 3:16; Romans 8:9; Galatians 5:22; Philippians 4:19. Then discuss the following question with your whole group. Ask:

- **What are the benefits of salvation in Jesus?**

TAKING ACTION:
Decision Time

Say:

It's now time to prayerfully consider all we've studied today. Remember that little gift I gave you at the beginning of class? It wasn't much, but for you to have it, you had to accept it from me. The same is true of salvation in Jesus. If you believe that the Bible's message about Jesus is true, maybe it's time for you to accept that message and make a faith commitment to Jesus. I'll be available after class to talk with anyone about any questions you have or decisions you've made. If you've made a decision, please be sure to let me know.

If you feel it's appropriate, you might want to pray a brief prayer of faith commitment, encouraging people who want to make that commitment to pray silently along with you. You also might want to send home with your class members something that explains God's plan of salvation so that they can think through it more fully on their own.

Close your session with prayer.

# *W*HAT'S A CHRISTIAN?

OPENING DISCUSSION

In your group, discuss the following quote from *Spiritual Entrepreneurs* by Michael Slaughter:
"I have visited many Sunday school classes when the people were…studying the lives of Abraham, Moses, David, or one of the other biblical characters. Information is given about 4,000-year-old people, and we feel that the purpose of the class has been accomplished. Scripture was not given for information. It was given that we might see the One who is the author of life and be radically transformed through him."

- How fully do you agree with the message of this statement?
- How does the Old Testament help us today?
- How does Jesus transform lives?

WHY JESUS CAME

For each question below, look up the passages and discuss the question that follows.

The Sin Problem

1. Isaiah 53:6; Romans 3:10; Romans 3:23; John 3:19

- *What have we humans done to create our own problems?*

2. Isaiah 59:2; Romans 6:23; Romans 14:12

- *What is the result of our actions?*

The Jesus Remedy

3. Isaiah 53:5; Romans 5:8-9; Titus 3:5; Ephesians 2:8-9

- *How did Jesus' coming help us?*

Repentance and Forgiveness

4. Isaiah 55:7; 1 John 1:9; John 1:12; Acts 16:31

- *What must we do to receive salvation in Jesus and enter into a personal relationship with him?*

5. Romans 5:1; Romans 8:1; 2 Corinthians 5:17

- *What does salvation in Jesus mean to us?*

The Lordship of Christ

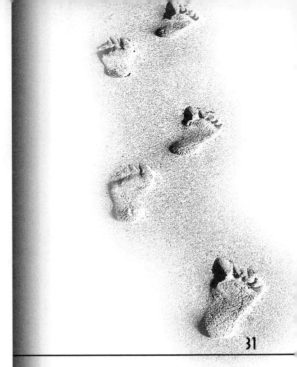

SESSION 4

BEFORE THE SESSION

Divide your meeting space into three sections by setting up three different circles of chairs around the room. Number the sections from 1 to 3, then carry out the following instructions for each section:

Section 1—Place several copies of the "Kingdom or Democracy?" handouts (p. 36) in the center of the circle.

Section 2—Place several copies of the "Bondservant or Volunteer?" handouts (p. 37) in the center of the circle, along with a clean cloth.

Section 3—Place several copies of the "Who Is in Control?" handouts (p. 38) in the center of the circle, along with a stack of index cards and pens.

OPENER:
Follow the Leader

As participants arrive, encourage them to sit in one of the three circles you've created. Once everyone has arrived and is seated, quietly go around the room and observe where each person has chosen to sit. Then go up to several people at random and tell them that you'd prefer it if they switch places with someone in another circle. Do not

SUPPLIES NEEDED:

- Bibles
- "Kingdom or Democracy?" handouts (p. 36)
- "Bondservant or Volunteer?" handouts (p. 37)
- "Who Is in Control?" handouts (p. 38)
- index cards
- pens
- clean cloth

offer any explanation as to why. After you've moved several people from their original spots, randomly ask a few participants to stand where they are. Again, offer no explanation. If they ask, just say that you need them to trust you. Once several people are standing, ask everyone to sit down and discuss these questions within their groups:

- **In general, how do you feel about being told what to do?**
- **What's your reaction to what I just did—telling you whether you should stand or where you should sit, without explanation?**
- **How is your reaction to this experience similar to the way we react to authority in general?**
- **Why is it sometimes hard for us to submit to authority?**

Say:

Today we're going to explore several areas related to authority in order to get us thinking about the implications of this profound fact: Jesus is Lord. We will explore the differences between kingdoms and democracies, explore the difference between a bondservant and a volunteer, and look at who is in control of our resources. We will use Scripture to guide our discussion in each area.

The circle in which you're sitting represents one of these areas of exploration. You will spend about ten minutes completing the handout I've placed in the center of your circle. Then I will instruct the groups to rotate so that your group can study another aspect of authority and control. We will continue until your group has had a chance to look at each of the three issues I have laid before you. As you go through each area, keep in mind that your ultimate goal is to answer the question "What does it mean to make Jesus Lord of my life?"

BIBLE EXPLORATION:
Circle Discussions

Have group members work together to complete the handouts you placed in the center of their circles. After about ten minutes (or when all the groups seem to be finished), instruct the groups to move to a different circle so that they can explore another aspect of authority and the Lordship of Christ. When the groups have gone through all three circles, have participants move the chairs to form one large circle. Then ask:

- **What did you discover about your group members during these discussions?**
- **What did you discover about yourself?**
- **How do you feel about the idea of Jesus as "Lord" over everything in your life?**
- **Practically speaking, what does it mean to make Jesus "Lord" of your life?**

Say:

To make Jesus "Lord" means to give him control over everything in our lives—all that we do, all that we own, even all that we think. In our affluent society and individualistic mentality, giving up *anything* is a major issue. We may have uncomfortable feelings and even fear in giving up control. But let's remember to whom we are giving control.

Read aloud Matthew 11:28-30. Then say:

Our trust in Jesus grows as we come to know him and understand his character and his loving intentions toward us.

BIBLE APPLICATION:
A Life of Dependence

Read the following statement aloud to the class: **Coming to Jesus is not just a continuation of life as it has been with the addition of God's blessing; rather, it is a life of obedience—doing what Jesus tells us to do. Obedience is more than lip service. It is a way of life in which we are no longer self-ruling individuals. Everything in our lives is ruled by God.**

Ask the following questions, allowing time after each one for discussion:

- **Do you agree with this statement? Why or why not?**

Have a volunteer read aloud Matthew 7:21-27. Then ask:

- **Why do you think Jesus wants to be Lord of your life?**
- **What benefits could you gain by relinquishing control of your life to God?**
- **What's the main thing that hinders you from letting Jesus be Lord of your life?**

Say:

Most of us are determined to be independent, making our own decisions, but if Jesus is Lord, who should be controlling our decisions? Who are we to obey? Listen to these words from John 14:15: "If you love me, you will obey what I command." Jesus makes it clear that to love him means to follow him with single-minded obedience.

TAKING ACTION:

Recognizing Jesus as Lord

Have participants move their chairs away from everyone else and sit quietly with their eyes closed. Say:

Let's take time to reflect on what has been said today. Recognize that as we accept Jesus and enter into relationship with him, we accept and relate to him as Savior and Lord. It comes as a package, not a two-step process. If Jesus is Lord, then he has absolute authority over all of my life. I can no longer compartmentalize it.

Please take a few minutes to be silent and allow the Lord Jesus to show you where you need to let him be Lord. As he shows you each area of your life that you need to let Jesus control, give it to him, and then silently pray for him to have complete authority in your life.

Note to the Leader: Before participants leave, this would be a good time to distribute to them information about your church's perspective on baptism and its role in salvation or church membership. Encourage participants to read the information before the next class and to write down any questions they may have about your church's views on this important step of faith.

KINGDOM OR DEMOCRACY?

In your small group, look over these descriptions of a kingdom and a democracy. Then discuss the questions that follow.

DEMOCRACY	KINGDOM
A democracy is headed by elected leaders who can be changed based on their popularity with people.	A king rules on the basis of his birth and is king for life.
A democracy allows participation by members of that democracy in the decision-making process. The people can change the rules.	A kingdom is ruled by a king who gives decrees and expects obedience. Approval by the people is not involved.
The leadership in a democracy represents the people.	In a kingdom the people represent the king.

- Based on these descriptions, is your home life more like a democracy or a kingdom? Explain.

- What about your work environment? Is it more like a democracy or a kingdom? Explain.

- Read these verses together: Luke 23:2-3; 1 Timothy 6:15; Acts 2:36; Acts 10:36; and Revelation 19:16. From these verses, is Christianity more like a democracy or a kingdom?

Read this statement together:
Jesus came as King of kings and Lord of lords, ruler over all. Being in relationship with him means joining his kingdom, putting us under his rule and authority. This requires obedience to his commands on our part.

BONDSERVANT OR VOLUNTEER?

In your small group, form pairs. In each pair, choose one person to be the Master and one to be the Servant. For the next three minutes, the Servants must do anything the Masters tell them to. The Servants may not talk unless asked to speak, nor may they do anything of their own volition. They may do only what their Masters command.

Here is a list of suggested commands for the Masters to give to their Servants:

• Give me [or someone else] a shoulder rub.

• Go get me a drink of water.

• Retie my shoes, then use a cloth to wipe them clean.

After three minutes, you may all become equals again. Talk about what just happened by discussing these questions:

• How did it feel to be a Servant? a Master?

• Why does the idea of being a servant sound negative to us?

• Do you think of yourself as a servant to God? Why or why not?

Have a volunteer read this aloud to the group:

The thought of being a servant or slave is not normally a pleasing one to us. Slavery or servanthood represents a loss of control over our lives. We like to say, "I volunteer my time at the church." But that's not really how the early disciples saw themselves.

Read together these verses: Philippians 1:1; James 1:1; Revelation 1:1; Philemon 1:1; and Titus 1:1.

• Do you think these disciples saw themselves as part-time volunteers in Christ's cause or as lifelong servants of Christ?

• Why is it important that we follow their example in serving God?

WHO IS IN CONTROL?

In your small group, have each person take an index card and a pen. On your card, write the five most valuable resources you possess. These may be material or financial possessions but could also include less tangible items such as time, talents, career, and family.

Next to each item, write the name of the person or institution that presently has authority and control over that resource. If it's a person who is the resource, that person may also be the authority. If it's time or talent, the authority may be you. When you have finished, share what you wrote on your card with the rest of your group.

When everyone has shared, read together Acts 2:42-47 and Acts 4:32-35. Discuss:

- What do these say about the way the early disciples viewed their personal resources?

- Based on these verses, who do you think was in control of the disciples' resources?

For each item on your card, cross out the name of the person or institution that you listed as being in control of that resource, and write "Jesus Christ" in its place. Then on the back of your card, write a description of how your life might be different if you gave Jesus total control of each of the resources you listed.

When you have finished, you may want to share what you wrote with the rest of your group. Don't pressure anyone to share who's uncomfortable with it.

A FOLLOWER'S
Life

SECTION 2

LIFE IN THE SPIRIT

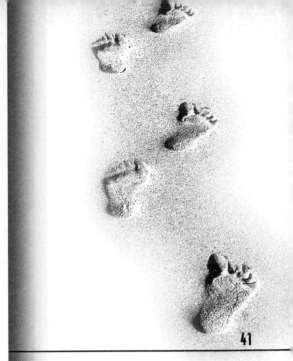

Who Is the Holy Spirit?

SESSION 5

BEFORE THE SESSION

A short time before class, put some water on to boil. When it reaches a boil, pour it into a thermos and seal the lid. Place a few trays of ice inside a small cooler. Take the items to the classroom, along with the rest of the supplies listed in the margin. Set up a small table in the front of the room. Set the boiled egg at one end, and the thermos and cooler at the other. Set three or four sheets of paper and a marker to one side.

OPENER:
Symbols of the Trinity

Once everyone has arrived, ask a volunteer to step to the front of the room. Ask him or her:

- **Are you a father** [or mother]? **a brother** [or sister]? **an employee?**

For each question to which the volunteer answers "yes," write that label on a separate sheet of paper, and tape it to the volunteer's clothing. If your volunteer has no job or has no siblings, create labels for other roles he or she plays, such as "son," "daughter," "friend," or "neighbor." The important thing is that you end up

SUPPLIES NEEDED:

- Bibles
- "Holy Spirit Personal Profile" handouts (p. 46)
- "Holy Spirit Job Description" handouts (p. 47)
- paper
- tape
- pens
- markers
- boiled egg
- boiling water
- thermos
- trays of ice
- cooler

Life IN THE SPIRIT

with three labels on the volunteer.

Once you've labeled the volunteer, open the thermos so that participants know that steaming water is in the thermos and the cooler lid so that the ice can be seen. Then say:

We're going to begin our session today with a riddle. Here we have a person with three labels, an egg, and two containers holding different forms of water. What do these three things have in common?

Invite responses from the participants. If no one guesses the answer, say:

The solution to the riddle is this: Each of these items is a model that helps us understand the Trinity, the mysterious "three in one" nature of God.

Most of us understand who God the Father is, who Jesus is, and the relationship between the two. However, when we add the Holy Spirit to the conversation, we sometimes become confused. These models help us understand how God can be Father, Son, and Holy Spirit—and yet remain one God.

Walk participants through a brief explanation of each model, describing for them how each model helps us understand God's three-in-one nature. A brief overview of each model is included here for your convenience:

1. Person with three roles—Your volunteer is one whole person, yet he or she plays different roles in life, depending on the circumstance. It is typical for a man to simultaneously act as a son, a father, and a brother. All three identities are true and coexist in one person. In the same way, God is One Being, yet plays different roles in his relationship with people.
2. The egg—The egg has three parts: the yolk, the white, and the shell. Yet it is still one egg. In the same way, God is One but has three parts.
3. The water in three forms—The chemical equation of water, H_2O, remains constant no matter what form the water takes. Ice, liquid water, and steam are all the same thing—even

though they are in different forms. In the same way, though consistently the same, God exists in three forms: Father, Son, and Holy Spirit.

Once everyone understands each model, say:

Today our goal is to answer both of those questions together:

• **Who is the Holy Spirit?**
• **What is his role in our lives?**

BIBLE EXPLORATION:
Holy Spirit Portfolio

Have participants form two groups, and give both groups a supply of paper and pens. Give each person in one group a copy of the "Holy Spirit Personal Profile" handout (p. 46). Give each person in the other group a copy of the "Holy Spirit Job Description" handout (p. 47). Tell group members that their job is to work together to complete their assigned handouts, all but the homework, and then prepare a presentation to teach the other group what they have learned.

When groups have completed their handouts, make sure everyone has a copy of both handouts. Then have groups take turns teaching each other what they learned about the Holy Spirit's nature and his role in the world.

Say:

The Holy Spirit is God, equal with the Father and the Son, and has all the attributes and power and wisdom that God possesses. The Holy Spirit is the Spirit of God, the Spirit of Christ. And if you are a Christian, the Holy Spirit lives within your spirit. It is essential to grasp the fact that the Spirit is a person so we understand that we can be in continual relationship with God through the Spirit. The Holy Spirit enables us to know and walk with God personally by being present, active, and responsive in the life of the believer.

43

44

Filled With the Spirit

Ask:

- **What do you think is the difference between "having" the Holy Spirit within us and "being filled" with the Spirit?**
- **Do you think there are Christians who are not "Spirit-filled"? Why or why not?**

Have a volunteer read aloud Acts 2:38 and Romans 8:9. Then say:

The definition of a Christian is one who has the Spirit of God, so every Christian has the Holy Spirit living within. Being filled with the Spirit, however, is a different matter.

Ask volunteers to read Acts 4:8-13; Acts 4:31-35; Galatians 5:16-18; and Galatians 5:22-25. Then have participants form pairs and discuss these questions:

- **What can you glean from these Scriptures about what it means to be "filled" with the Holy Spirit?**
- **What happens when we are filled with the Holy Spirit?**
- **Why do you think it's important to be continually filled with the Holy Spirit?**

After the discussion, ask volunteers to share some of their responses with the whole group. Then say:

Becoming filled with the Holy Spirit is accomplished when we choose to give up control over our own lives and allow the Holy Spirit to lead and empower us. To be filled with the Holy Spirit is to be filled with Christ.

TAKING ACTION:
Pursuing the Spirit-Filled Life

Say:

Being filled with the Holy Spirit establishes Jesus as Lord of our lives. Let's pray together to ask the Spirit to fill us, to empower us to be all that God intended us to be.

Have participants form a circle and join hands. Pray together, allowing participants to pray aloud or silently, asking God's Spirit to fill them and take control of their lives. After a few minutes, close the prayer time by praying for God's Spirit to fill each person in the class. If possible, call out each participant by name.

After the prayer, remind participants that being filled with the Spirit is not a one-time event but a daily act of obedience. Encourage them to pray for God's Spirit to fill them every day as they commit themselves to obeying God in everything they do.

# Holy Spirit Personal Profile

Your goal as a group is to create a personal profile of the Holy Spirit—a description of who he is and his personality traits. Use the following Scriptures and questions as your guide.

Basic Attributes

1. **Read Romans 8:27.** What attribute of the Holy Spirit does this passage describe?

2. **Read 1 Corinthians 2:10-13.** What attribute of the Holy Spirit does this passage describe?

3. **Read 1 Corinthians 12:11.** What attribute of the Holy Spirit does this passage describe?

4. **Read Matthew 28:19; 2 Corinthians 13:14; John 14:16-18; and Romans 8:9.** Based on these Scriptures, do you think the Holy Spirit should be equated with God? Why or why not?

Personality Traits

5. Based on the following Scriptures, write a brief description of the Holy Spirit's personality: John 14:16-17; 1 Corinthians 12:4-11; and Galatians 5:22-25.

HOLY SPIRIT JOB DESCRIPTION

Your goal as a group is to create a job description for the Holy Spirit—an overview of the Holy Spirit's role in the world and the lives of Christians. Read each of the following Scriptures. Next to each one, write the aspect of the Holy Spirit's job that the passage describes.

• John 14:25-26; John 16:13	
• John 15:16	
• John 16:8-11	
• Romans 8:16	
• Acts 1:8	
• 1 Corinthians 6:19	
• 1 Corinthians 12:7	
• Galatians 5:16-18	

Homework

Write a classified ad as if it were for someone to fill the Holy Spirit's role. Include everything you can think of that describes what the Holy Spirit does.

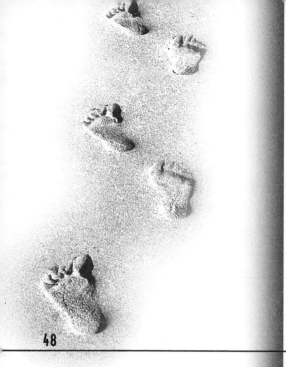

Lifestyle in the Spirit

SESSION 6

SUPPLIES NEEDED:

- Bibles
- "Fruit of the Spirit" handouts (pp. 52-53)
- "Evaluating Your Fruit" handouts (pp. 54-55)
- "Fruit of the Spirit Response Sheet" handouts (p. 56)
- pens
- three or four large salad bowls
- three or four cutting boards and knives
- table
- serving spoons
- small bowls
- spoons
- napkins
- water and cups

For the opening activity, you'll need:

- nine plates
- nine different types of fruit
  (such as: apples, oranges, pears, bananas, grapes, kiwis, pineapples, peaches, and cantaloupe)

BEFORE THE SESSION

You'll need to set up nine "fruit" stations around the meeting room. A station can simply be a chair covered in a towel or sheet. At each station, place a handful of pens, some napkins, and one section of the "Fruit of the Spirit" handout (pp. 52-53). Place a platter of fruit next to each station—a different fruit for each station. Wash the fruit beforehand, but do not cut it up or prepare it in any way.

For added effect, you could place a few lighted candles at each station and dim the room lights. You might also consider playing soft instrumental music in the background while participants go through the stations.

OPENER:

Why Fruit Matters

Once everyone has arrived, have participants gather in the center of the room—away from the fruit stations, if possible. Then say:

In our last session, we discussed the person of the Holy Spirit and the Spirit's role in our lives. One of the key words we touched on last week was what the Bible calls spiritual "fruit." As you may have suspected, this week we're going to explore that idea more in depth and

discover what it means to bear spiritual fruit.

Ask volunteers to take turns reading aloud John 15:1-8; Luke 6:43-45; and Galatians 5:22-23. Then say:

As you can see, there is an expectation that "fruit" will be produced in the life of a Christian. The fruit of the Spirit described in Galatians 5:22 is not something we receive as a one-time event. It is progressively produced in us through a life that is consistently yielded to the Holy Spirit. It is the work of the Holy Spirit, not something we produce in our own strength. However, it does not happen without our cooperation. We have to make conscious choices to continually submit ourselves to God and to obey every day. As we yield to the Spirit in this way, the fruit of the Spirit will grow and mature so that in time, we begin to look more and more like Jesus.

Let's embark together on a journey to discover what the fruit of the Spirit looks like and how we can begin to develop that fruit in our lives.

BIBLE EXPLORATION:

Journey of Discovery

Have participants form three or four groups, and give each group a knife, a cutting board, and a large salad bowl. (If you have more than twenty-five people in your class, you might consider forming five or six groups instead.) Make sure participants have their Bibles, then send each group to a different station in the room. At each station have a different member of the group share an answer to the question on the handout. It doesn't matter at which station each group begins, and they may go through the stations in any order they wish.

If you have brought instrumental music, begin to play it in the background as groups begin their journey.

While groups are working, quietly set up a table and set out the small bowls, spoons, and napkins. Prepare a glass of water for each person.

BIBLE APPLICATION:
Evaluating the Fruit

When all the groups have finished, have them bring their newly made fruit salads to the table, and place a large serving spoon in each one. Serve each participant a bowl of the fruit salad made by his or her group. Then have everyone sit down.

As participants are enjoying the fruit salad, ask:

- **How is the makeup of this salad like the fruit of the Spirit in our lives?**
- **How is it like the church?**

Say:

Most of us know how to evaluate fruits to tell whether they are good or bad to eat. Well, there is also a way to evaluate how well we express the fruit of the Spirit in our lives. As you enjoy this fruit of the earth, let's take some time to evaluate the fruit of the Spirit in our own lives.

Give each participant a pen and a copy of the "Evaluating Your Fruit" handout (pp. 54-55). As they eat, have them complete the handout. When they have finished, give each person a "Fruit of the Spirit Response Sheet" (p. 56) so that they can gauge their effectiveness at expressing the fruit of the Spirit.

TAKING ACTION:
Bearing Good Fruit

When participants have completed the "Fruit of the Spirit Response Sheet," have them form pairs and share their results with their partners. Have participants use their pens to circle one aspect of the spiritual fruit in which they are strong and one that needs work. Then have partners pray for each other, thanking God for displaying fruit in them and asking for the Holy Spirit to work through them to display fruit more powerfully in their lives.

HOMEWORK

For this week's homework, have people do a spiritual gifts assessment. Many such assessments are available and can be purchased through a bookstore or on the Internet. We recommend *Breakthru: A Spiritual Gifts Diagnostic Inventory* by Ralph Ennis. You may obtain this tool from LEAD Consulting, P. O. Box 3206, Raleigh, NC 27622. Their phone number is (919) 783-0354, and their Web site is lead.wilmington.org (no www).

51

FRUIT OF THE SPIRIT

Photocopy this handout, and cut it into sections. Place each section at a different fruit station.

---

1. *Love:* the ability to unconditionally accept and love others based in this same quality offered to us by God through Jesus Christ; the ability to give ourselves in service to others without expecting anything in return.

As you read through these Scriptures, prepare some of the fruit at this station, and place it in your bowl.

Luke 6:35	John 13:34-35	1 Corinthians 13:4-7
John 3:16	1 John 4:19-21	

How have you seen this kind of love demonstrated?

---

2. *Joy:* a deep, inner gladness that results from an intimate relationship with Christ. It is maintained through obedience and is renewed through service to others. Joy is not dependent on circumstances but springs from our communion with God.

As you read through these Scriptures, prepare some of the fruit at this station, and place it in your bowl.

John 15:10-11	Acts 13:52	Romans 15:13
John 17:13	Romans 14:17-18	

Share a time you've experienced this joy even when you've not been happy.

---

3. *Peace:* an inner harmony and sense of well being, based on our confident faith that God has accepted us, loves us, and is in control of our lives no matter how turbulent our external situation might be.

As you read through these Scriptures, prepare some of the fruit at this station, and place it in your bowl.

Isaiah 32:17	Philippians 4:4-7	Acts 13:52
John 16:33	Romans 5:1	

When have you experienced God's peace?

---

4. *Patience:* the ability to exercise restraint and calmly persevere in waiting on God, despite people or circumstances that might provoke us or cause agitation.

As you read through these Scriptures, prepare some of the fruit at this station, and place it in your bowl.

1 Corinthians 13:4	2 Timothy 4:2	1 Thessalonians 5:14
Colossians 3:12-13	Ephesians 4:2	

Where in your life do you need this fruit?

---

5. *Kindness:* the ability to treat others with openness, sensitivity, and love—especially those who have specific needs we can meet. This ability is based on the kindness shown to us by God.

As you read through these Scriptures, prepare some of the fruit at this station, and place it in your bowl.

Romans 2:4	2 Peter 1:5-8	Ephesians 4:2
Ephesians 2:6-7	Romans 11:22	

Share a time you've experienced the undeserved kindness of another.

---

6. *Goodness:* to have the nature of God, and therefore to be able to discern right from wrong, do good to others, and expose evil and injustice.

As you read through these Scriptures, prepare some of the fruit at this station, and place it in your bowl.

Matthew 19:17	Mark 10:18
Romans 15:14	Ephesians 5:8-11

What example can you give of goodness in action?

---

7. *Faithfulness:* an unshakable loyalty displayed by being trustworthy, reliable, and responsible; completely carrying out commitments to God and others.

As you read through these Scriptures, prepare some of the fruit at this station, and place it in your bowl.

Matthew 23:23-24	3 John 3	Hebrews 10:23
1 Corinthians 4:1-2, 17	Matthew 25:21	

How have you seen the faithfulness of God through others?

---

8. *Gentleness:* demonstrating consideration and thoughtfulness; putting my rights and strength willingly under God's control in order to seek peace in a calm manner. Gentleness requires openness, humility, and a teachable spirit, rather than the harshness originating from personal pride and selfishness.

As you read through these Scriptures, prepare some of the fruit at this station, and place it in your bowl.

Matthew 11:29	Titus 3:1-2	1 Timothy 6:1
Ephesians 4:2-3	1 Corinthians 4:21	

Who in your life demonstrates gentleness?

---

9. *Self-control:* to take authority over oneself and exercise discipline in order to avoid sin and live a life that pleases God.

As you read through these Scriptures, prepare some of the fruit at this station, and place it in your bowl.

1 Corinthians 6:12	2 Peter 1:5-6	Titus 1:8
2 Timothy 3:3-5	1 Corinthians 7:5	

Where do you need increased self-control?

EVALUATING YOUR FRUIT

Based on your personal experience, respond to the following statements. Use the number system below to rank each statement.

0—Never true for me   2—True most of the time

1—True every once in a while   3—Definitely true for me

____ 1. I am grateful that God loved the world (and me!) so much that he gave his Son.

____ 2. God's presence makes me glad.

____ 3. I rest in the fact that God is in control of all things—past, present, and future.

____ 4. Even though I don't always understand what's happening, I am willing to wait on God to act on my behalf.

____ 5. I am amazed by God's intense care for me shown by sending Jesus to take the punishment I deserve.

____ 6. I know that there are times God is justified in being angry.

____ 7. I love the fact that Jesus set aside his power as God in order to reach out to the broken and hurting.

____ 8. I know that God will do exactly what he says he will do.

____ 9. My lifestyle reflects my obedience to God.

____ 10. I'm confident in God's love for me, even when I act in an unloving way toward others.

____ 11. I have an inner assurance of my relationship with Jesus.

____ 12. Because I have Jesus, I am calmer, even when problems come along.

____ 13. I accept others right where they are.

____ 14. I choose to forgive others because Jesus chooses to forgive me.

____ 15. I am immediately sensitive to the conviction of God's Spirit when I've done something wrong.

____ 16. When someone approaches me in anger, I generally don't react with the same harshness.

____ 17. People who know me well would say that I have a consistent walk with God.

____ 18. I say "no" to things that might hinder my communion with God.

____ 19. I am committed to serving others, even when I don't feel like it.

____ 20. Even when things go wrong, I have an inner assurance of God's presence.

____ 21. I am confident that my sins are forgiven.

____ 22. I don't complain about my problems; instead, I trust God.

____ 23. I comfort, encourage, and affirm others.

____ 24. I live a lifestyle that pleases God.

____ 25. Even when I feel attacked, I am committed to obeying God's Word and submitting to the Holy Spirit.

____ 26. I follow through with what I say I will do.

____ 27. I am committed to a consistent time alone with God for prayer and Bible study.

____ 28. I choose to be positive and affirm the good qualities of people, even when they get on my nerves.

____ 29. I have consistent satisfaction from doing what God wants me to do.

_____ 30. I am confident that God accepts me because of my relationship with Jesus.

_____ 31. I am content that God has me in process and will develop me into what he wants me to be.

_____ 32. I speak positively to others to build them up.

_____ 33. I am truthful, honest, and keep the promises I make.

_____ 34. I seek to be humble, cooperative, and teachable all the time.

_____ 35. I am responsible.

_____ 36. I have asked my friends or a support group to hold me accountable for areas in which I struggle.

_____ 37. I serve others with no expectation of being served in return.

_____ 38. I have a deep sense of pleasure because I sense God's presence as I serve.

_____ 39. I am not easily stressed out because I know God is in control.

_____ 40. I am willing to wait for things that will benefit me physically, spiritually, or materially.

_____ 41. I listen and try to understand others.

_____ 42. I have confronted other Christians in a caring way when they have made wrong choices in the way they live.

_____ 43. I am open and receptive to feedback in areas in which I need improvement.

_____ 44. I use the abilities God has given me for his glory.

_____ 45. When I recognize a behavior problem in my life, I immediately act to bring it under control.

_____ 46. When I have been hurt, I am willing to forgive and begin again with that person.

_____ 47. I delight in what God is doing in the lives of others.

_____ 48. I have a calm assurance even in difficult situations.

_____ 49. When I am hurting, I place my hope in God.

_____ 50. I am compassionate and respond to the needs of others.

_____ 51. I am involved in serving others in my community and around the world in order to influence others for Jesus.

_____ 52. Regardless of my feelings, I focus on doing what is right.

_____ 53. Because I belong to God, I understand that my time, money, and energy are his to use as he wishes.

_____ 54. Distractions do not keep me from my goals.

_____ 55. I pray for my enemies and for those who are difficult to love.

_____ 56. No matter what I am doing, I am content because God is with me and is using me to serve others.

_____ 57. I experience the Holy Spirit's comfort in the midst of the world's chaos.

_____ 58. I accept others who are different from me.

_____ 59. I treat others with kindness and generosity, even when they are different from me or rejected by others.

_____ 60. I take a stand for truth and against injustice.

_____ 61. I don't seek revenge when others hurt me.

_____ 62. My friends know they can count on me.

_____ 63. I stay away from situations in which I am easily tempted.

Permission to photocopy this handout from *A Follower's Life* granted for local church use. Copyright © Carolyn Slaughter and Sheryl K. Douglas. Published by Group Publishing, Inc., P.O. Box 481, Loveland, CO 80539. www.grouppublishing.com

FRUIT OF THE SPIRIT RESPONSE SHEET

Transfer the answers from your questions to the corresponding numbers on this response sheet. Be sure to follow the numbers correctly, noting that they go in columns vertically. Once you have done this, add the scores in each horizontal line. For example, for line A (Love), you will add up the responses to the statements 1, 10, 19, 28, 37, 46, and 55. Place your totals in the column marked "Total."

There is a total possible score of 21 for each aspect of the fruit of the Spirit. The higher you score for each quality, the more likely you are to be demonstrating that quality in your life.

For a more complete evaluation, have your close friends and loved ones complete the test as well, answering each question according to how strongly they see the fruit of the Spirit displayed through your life.

							TOTAL	FRUIT
A:1	10	19	28	37	46	55	A	Love
B:2	11	20	29	38	47	56	B	Joy
C:3	12	21	30	39	48	57	C	Peace
D:4	13	22	31	40	49	58	D	Patience
E:5	14	23	32	41	50	59	E	Kindness
F:6	15	24	33	42	51	60	F	Goodness
G:7	16	25	34	43	52	61	G	Gentleness
H:8	17	26	35	44	53	62	H	Faithfulness
I:9	18	27	36	45	54	63	I	Self-Control

Understanding Spiritual Gifts

SESSION 7

BEFORE THE SESSION
Make photocopies of the handouts for your class members.

OPENER:
Fruits and Gifts

Welcome everyone to the class, then begin your class time with prayer. After the prayer, say:

> **In our last session we focused on the fruit of the Spirit. In this session we're going to look at a different aspect of the spiritual life: spiritual gifts. Before we begin, I'd like us to understand the difference between spiritual fruit and a spiritual gift.**

On one sheet of newsprint, create a chart with two columns. Title the left side "Fruit" and the right side "Gifts." Ask participants to help you fill in the left side of the chart with facts about the nature of spiritual fruit. For example, the fruit of the Spirit
- is the same in every Christian.
- deals with character.
- develops through a journey.
- is a goal for every Christian.
- helps define what a Christian is.
- cannot be imitated by Satan.

SUPPLIES NEEDED:
- "Defining Spiritual Gifts" handouts (pp. 62-63)
- "Spiritual Journey Worksheet" handouts (p. 67)
- newsprint
- markers
- paper
- pens

Life IN THE SPIRIT

In the right column, challenge participants to come up with contrasting statements that they think might describe spiritual gifts. For example, spiritual gifts

- are different for every Christian.
- deal with service and ministry.
- are given at conversion.
- are a means to reach God's goal for the church.
- help determine what a Christian does.
- can be imitated by Satan.

Once the list is complete, ask:

- **Now that we can see some of the differences between fruit and gifts, why do you think God gave us spiritual gifts?**

After several people have responded, ask a volunteer to read aloud Ephesians 4:12-16. Then say:

Spiritual gifts are special abilities given by the Holy Spirit to equip and build up the Body of Christ. Although spiritual gifts are given by God *to you*, the gifts God gives you are not *for you*. They are for the church. They are essentially tools God gives you so you can build up and serve others. In addition, it's important to keep in mind that spiritual gifts are not marks of maturity in Christ. Having a spiritual gift doesn't mean you have "arrived" spiritually. Far from it! Rather, maturity is measured by how well we express the fruit of the Spirit in our lives.

With that in mind, let's examine what the gifts are and see if we can determine which gifts God may have given us.

BIBLE EXPLORATION:
What Are the Gifts?

Have each participant use a marker to write his or her signature on a sheet of paper. Then have participants write their signatures again on the same papers, this time using the opposite hand.

After the experience, have everyone hold up their signatures for others to see. Ask:

- **How did it feel to do something that was not natural to you?**
- **What was the result of your efforts?**
- **Have you ever tried to serve the church in some way that was not natural to you?**
- **If so, what was the result? If not, what do you think would happen if you did?**

Say:

God has created you in a unique way and has prepared you to serve within the church. Part of this preparation is giving you one or more spiritual gifts. But not all of our gifts are the same. God has not used a cookie cutter to stamp out people in a process of uniformity. That's why it feels awkward for you to serve the Body of Christ in some way that doesn't suit your spiritual gifts.

But what is a spiritual gift, anyway? It is a supernatural power within you to serve others. It is more than a human talent; it is the work of the Holy Spirit in your life, empowering you in a specific way to serve well. Let's take some time to define each of the gifts the Bible names.

Ask a volunteer to read aloud Romans 12:6-8; 1 Corinthians 12:4-11, 27-31; and Ephesians 4:11-13. As the volunteer reads, make a list on newsprint of all the spiritual gifts highlighted in the passages. Afterward, say:

As you heard, some gifts are listed more than once and others just once. Altogether there are twenty different gifts mentioned within the three Scripture references. Let's explore these twenty in more detail.

Have participants form six groups, and give each person a pen and a copy of the "Defining Spiritual Gifts" handout (pp. 62-63). Have each group complete only one section of the handout. Then have groups take turns sharing with the rest of the class what they discovered about their assigned gifts.

After every group has shared its findings, say:

It's important not only to understand what the gifts are, but also which specific gifts God has given you. Identifying your own spiritual gifts can really help you find your place of service within the Body of Christ.

BIBLE APPLICATION:
My Gifts

Have each person take a few minutes to read through the definitions and examples for each of the gifts. Then, using a pen and the results of their gifts survey (from the homework), have each person circle each of the gifts he or she has identified.

When everyone has finished, have participants form pairs and share with their partners which gifts they circled. Have partners pray together, asking God to reveal and confirm the gifts he has given to each of them and show them specific ways they can use those gifts to serve his people.

After the prayer, say:

How can you be sure you know which gifts God has given you? First, listen to your own heart. God often reveals his will through our inner desires and passions. We will have excitement, joy, and anticipation for serving in our gifted area. You will feel fulfilled when functioning in the area intended for you. Second, listen to those Christians closest to you. Often, God will confirm your suspicions about which gifts you have through the observations and opinions of mature Christians God has placed in your life.

TAKING ACTION:
Testing the Waters

Say:

> **The third way you can be certain whether or not God has given you a particular spiritual gift is to test it. And that's exactly what I'd like you to do this week. Draw a star next to one of the gifts you circled on your handout. Then work with your partner to come up with one way you can test that gift this week. For example, if you think you have the gift of exhortation, you could write and send several encouraging cards or letters to your family members or friends. Examine the impact of your efforts. Since spiritual gifts are designed to benefit others, you should see positive results as you use your gifts. If you see no results when you experiment with a particular gift, you probably don't have that gift. But that's OK because there is a whole list of gifts to explore!**

As pairs finish, encourage them to call one another this week to see how the "gift testing" is going. When everyone has finished, give each person a copy of the "Spiritual Journey Worksheet" handout (p. 67), and encourage participants to complete the handout this week.

DEFINING SPIRITUAL GIFTS

For each of your assigned gifts, read the definition and the related Scriptures. Then, below each definition, write one way you might see that gift operating in the local church.

GROUP 1

Exhortation (encouragement)—the ability to encourage people and assist them in moving toward spiritual maturity and personal wholeness. This gift uses the skills of comfort and confrontation, encouragement and instruction. (Romans 12:8)

Giving—the ability to give of material wealth freely and with joy to further God's causes. Use of this gift provides physical resources in response to assessed needs. (Romans 12:6-8)

Leadership—the ability to see "the big picture" and assemble the component parts through the ability to motivate, coordinate, and direct the efforts of others in doing God's work. (Romans 12:6-8)

GROUP 2

Teaching—the ability to understand and clearly communicate God's truths to others in ways that lead them to apply God's truth to their lives. (Ephesians 4:11-13)

Prophecy—the ability to proclaim God's truth in a way that's relevant to current situations and to envision how God would will things to change. (Ephesians 4:7, 11)

Mercy—the ability to perceive the suffering of others and comfort and minister effectively with empathy and without condemnation. (Romans 12:6-8)

GROUP 3

Serving—demonstrating God's love through the ability to identify the needs of others and selflessly working to meet them. (Romans 12:6-8)

Wisdom—the ability to understand and apply biblical and spiritual knowledge to practical, everyday problems. (1 Corinthians 12:7-8)

Knowledge—the ability to understand, organize, and effectively use information, from either natural sources or the Holy Spirit directly, for the advancement of God's purposes. (1 Corinthians 12:7-8)

GROUP 4

Faith—the ability to recognize what God wants to accomplish and the steadfast confidence that God will see it done despite what others perceive as barriers. (1 Corinthians 12:7, 9)

Healing—the ability to effectively call on God for the curing of illness and the restoration of health in a supernatural way. (1 Corinthians 12:7, 9)

Discernment of spirits—the ability to recognize what is of God and what is not of God. (1 Corinthians 12:7, 10)

Helps—the ability to work alongside others and see the value of accomplishing practical and often behind-the-scenes tasks that promote God's kingdom. (1 Corinthians 12:28)

GROUP 5

Speaking in tongues—the ability to supernaturally speak in a language, known or unknown to others, with no prior knowledge of that language. (1 Corinthians 12:7, 10)

Interpretation of tongues—the ability to understand and communicate the words of others who have spoken in tongues, even though the language is unknown. (1 Corinthians 12:7, 10)

Pastoring (shepherding)—the ability to guide and care for a group of Christians as they experience spiritual growth. (Ephesians 4:7, 11)

GROUP 6

Miracles—the ability to effectively call on God to do supernatural acts that glorify him. (1 Corinthians 12:7-8, 10)

Administration—the ability to organize information, events, or material to work efficiently for the Body of Christ. (1 Corinthians 12:28)

Apostleship—the ability to see the overall picture and respond by starting new churches, pioneering new ministries that impact multiple churches, or ministering transculturally. (Ephesians 4:7, 11)

Evangelism—the desire and ability to share the gospel with those who don't know him in a way that provokes them to believe in God. (Ephesians 4:7-11)

Sharing Your Spiritual Journey

SESSION 8

SUPPLIES NEEDED:

- Bibles
- "Spiritual Journey Worksheet" handouts (p. 67)
- pens
- bread
- juice or wine
- Communion supplies
- several large candles
- matches

BEFORE THE SESSION

On a table, set out the bread and juice or wine for Communion. Depending on your church's traditions regarding Communion, you may need to ask your pastor or some other member of the pastoral staff to join you for this session and lead the class in sharing Communion.

OPENER:

Your Spiritual Journey

Have participants form one large circle of chairs and sit down. Light a candle, and hold it in front of you. Say:

> **We have shared quite a lot in the last several weeks. We have gotten to know one another, have learned together, eaten together, accepted one another, and have become a community. Before we continue, we need to share another experience together. In this session, we will share with one another our individual spiritual journeys with Christ. For some of us, it will be a very short journey because we are new Christians or are even still considering whether or not to become a Christian. For others, the journey will**

cover a longer period of time. But each journey is exciting and heartwarming in its own way.

Give each person a pen, and ask participants to pull out the "Spiritual Journey Worksheet" handout that you asked them to complete last week. If some people don't have a worksheet, that's OK. Give them a copy, and ask them to complete it right now. Encourage them to create rough outlines on their handouts, rather than try to answer each question in detail. When they've finished, have participants form groups of eight or fewer, and give each group a lighted candle.

GROUP EXPLORATION:
Our Stories

Say:

In your groups, each person will share for three or four minutes from the "Spiritual Journey Worksheet" you have completed. Remember to stay focused on how learning about Jesus or becoming a Christian has transformed your life. Our lives before Christ can be shared, but it is not necessary to go into intimate details. Instead, talk about the impact Christ has had on your life.

When everyone is ready, have participants take turns sharing their stories within their groups. To help this process start well, you might ask a co-leader or older Christian to start the sharing in each group. Have each group member hold the candle while he or she shares and then pass it on to someone else.

GROUP APPLICATION:
Communion

When groups have finished, collect the candles, and have participants gather around the Communion table. Say:

We have shared our journeys. And to complete our time together, we will share another intimate experience: Communion.

Guide the class through Communion using the method preferred by your church. If you've invited a church leader to administer Communion to your group, encourage him or her to share the meaning of Communion for Christians and its significance for the class members.

TAKING ACTION:
A Prayer of Blessing

When the Communion time is finished, close your time together by having class members form groups of four or five and pray as a group for each person in their group. One way to do this is to set a chair in the center of the group and invite someone to sit in it. Then ask the rest of the group members to take turns praying aloud for that person's needs and thanking God for his or her presence in the group. Continue this process until the group has prayed for each person.

SPIRITUAL JOURNEY WORKSHEET

1. As you prepare to share your spiritual journey with your classmates, it will help you to organize your thoughts by writing what you want to say. Begin by sharing about your life before you became a Christian (or before you learned about who Jesus is). It is not necessary to give intimate details of your past; rather, focus on the events or feelings that have compelled you to search for truth.

2. Now write how you came to a faith relationship with Christ.

3. Finally, describe how God has changed you and what God is doing in your life today. If you are not yet a Christian, share how learning about Christ has impacted you personally and what you think is keeping you from deciding to become a Christian now.

SECTION 3

LIFE IN COMMUNITY

Keys to God's Heart

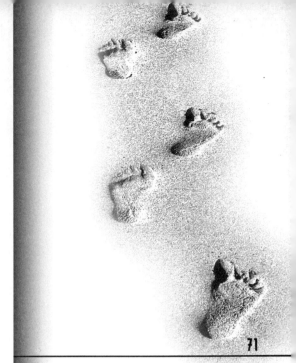

SESSION 9

BEFORE THE SESSION

Several weeks before this session, invite mature Christians to be members of a panel to discuss "Keys to God's Heart" (spiritual disciplines) and the impact of one or more of these keys on their lives. It's important for the panel members to be able to effectively communicate their experiences to the class. They should be willing to share openly about their struggles and victories, as well as how the Lord used a key to transform them. Ask each panel member to prepare a five-minute presentation. They all need a willingness to answer questions from the class. Remember, the panel is not to list "how to's" but to share personal experiences of the way Jesus was able to change them through the process of a particular key. Suggested "keys" are Bible study, prayer, and tithing. Additional keys could include fasting, worshiping, serving, journaling, and sharing faith with others. One other important key—fellowship in community with other Christians—will be covered in depth in the next session.

OPENER:

Keys to My Life

Have participants form groups of four to six, and ask everyone to pull out his or her keys. One at a time, have participants tell their

SUPPLIES NEEDED:

- Bibles
- paper
- pens

Life IN COMMUNITY

group what two or three of their keys open or operate and why each key is important to them. Afterward, say:

We don't often think much about keys, but they are clearly important for us to have in order to get where we need to go and do what we need to do each day. If you've ever lost your keys, you know exactly what I mean.

The same principle is true in our spiritual lives. Through the Bible, God teaches us about specific "keys" that we need to have in order to get where we need to go spiritually. These are keys to God's heart. We're going to learn about some of these keys today.

BIBLE EXPLORATION:
Keys to Intimacy With Jesus

With your whole class together, read aloud Jeremiah 29:13. Then ask:

• **What does it mean to seek God with all your heart?**

Say:

The keys to God's heart are a means to an end—intimacy with Jesus. The abundance of the Christian life flows from our intimacy with Jesus. To reach this intimacy, we must have internal discipline. *Webster's New World Dictionary* **defines** *discipline* **as "training that develops self-control." Internal discipline is the ability to choose God's way. It involves a series of choices we make to allow God to control our natures and develop us into what he wants us to be. It is something we decide to do and work at; it doesn't happen automatically.**

Have participants each turn to a partner and discuss these questions:

• **Why do you think God set up the Christian life so that we have to be disciplined in order to grow spiritually?**

Why didn't he make spiritual growth automatic?

• **When you were young, did your parents teach you to live a disciplined life? Explain.**

• **As an adult, are you now glad that your parents disciplined** [or didn't discipline] **you? Why or why not?**

• **What does your response say about the value of discipline in personal growth? in spiritual growth?**

Have pairs read Hebrews 12:10-11 together. Then ask:

• **Why is discipline essential to spiritual growth?**

Read Jeremiah 29:13 again. Then say:

We may want to know God passionately, but without a focus for that passion—without a way to direct it, hone it, and point it toward God's heart—our passion can quickly dissolve into a vague sentimentality. The keys to God's heart give us the focus and direction our passion needs. The keys are spiritual disciplines that help us know God.

We have invited several people here today to share with you their methods for knowing God's heart. Each of them will explain how they have come to know Jesus intimately. We asked each of them to focus on one or two areas so that each of the major spiritual disciplines will be addressed. If you want to know Jesus, truly know him, you will want to walk where these people walk.

BIBLE APPLICATION:
Panel Presentation and Discussion

Introduce each person, and tell which key(s) will be presented. Allow five to six minutes for each presentation. After all the panel members have shared, invite questions and discussion from the class. Be sure to provide paper and pens to class members so that they can take notes if they wish.

TAKING ACTION:
Personal Reflection

After the panel discussion, say to the class:

> **Now that you have heard how these Christian men and women have come to know Jesus, please take some time individually to reflect on what you've learned. What did you hear that you believe God can use in your life? Where do you need to start? On the paper I've given you, write at least one key that God wants you to begin using to transform your life.**

When participants have finished, close your time together with prayer. After the session, invite class members to talk one-on-one with panel members about any issues related to the discussion time.

Organism or Organization?

SESSION 10

BEFORE THE SESSION

Prepare a brief presentation that explains the organizational structure of your local church. Be sure to include information regarding the role of the pastor, the pastoral staff, the worship services, cell groups, and any other information your participants may find relevant to understanding how your church is organized. If you prefer, you may ask a member of the pastoral team to join you for this session so that he or she can make the presentation or answer any questions participants may have about your church's organization or ministry.

OPENER:

In His Image

Open class with prayer. Then say:

> **Today we're going to talk about the nature and purpose of the church. Together we're going to discover what exactly the church is and why it is here. To begin, I'd like to read a quote from the book *In His Image* by Dr. Paul Brand and Philip Yancey.**

Read aloud the quote on page 76.

SUPPLIES NEEDED:

- Bibles
- "What and Why?" handouts (p. 80)
- newsprint
- tape
- markers
- pens
- index cards

"Jesus, the exact likeness of God in flesh, expressed the image of God in human form. But from the very beginning he warned that his physical presence was temporary. He had in mind a further goal: to restore the broken image of God in humanity.

"God's activity on earth did not end with Jesus, and his image on earth did not vanish when Jesus departed. New Testament authors extend the term to a new Body God is creating composed of 'members'—men and women joining together to do the work of God. In referring to this Body, these writers pointedly use the same word that first described the spark of the divine in man and later described Christ. We are called, said Paul, to be 'the likeness [image] of his Son, that he might be the firstborn among many brothers' (Romans 8:29b)."

After reading the quote, have participants turn to a partner to discuss these questions:

- **What spoke to you from this quote?**
- **What is the difference between an organization and an organism?**
- **How do you see the church: primarily as an organization or an organism? Explain.**

Say:

The church is supposed to be organized, but it is not just an organization. It is an organism—a living representation of Christ here on earth. It's not a perfect representation by any means because it is filled with imperfect people like you and me. But it's through just such "broken vessels" that God chooses to reveal himself to the world.

Read aloud 2 Corinthians 4:6-7. Then say:

Let's learn more about what it means to be the body of Christ.

BIBLE EXPLORATION:
What and Why?

Have participants form two groups, and give each group a large sheet of newsprint, tape, markers, pens, and a copy of the "What and Why?" handout (p. 80). Assign each group a different section of the handout. Then say:

> **Your goal as a group is to create a mural that answers the question you've been assigned—either "What is the Church?" or "Why is the Church here?" Use the Scriptures provided to answer your question, then work together to create a visual representation of the answer. The mural can include symbols, words, or pictures. Don't worry about the quality of the "art." The goal is to communicate your answer visually—not to win any religious art awards.**

Encourage each group member to participate in the experience by reading Scriptures aloud, offering opinions, suggesting mural ideas, or drawing a portion of the mural.

When groups have finished, have them take turns presenting their murals. Then congratulate groups on their insight and creativity, and have participants form pairs by joining with members of the other group. Have partners discuss these questions:

- **Is the definition of the church what you expected it to be? Why or why not?**
- **How is the biblical definition of the church different from the way the rest of the world views the church?**
- **Based on what you've learned, do you think the church is currently fulfilling its purpose well? Why or why not?**
- **What can you do personally to help the church recognize what it is and do what it's supposed to do?**

Say:

We are the church. In order for the church to recognize its role in the world, we must each personally discover and fulfill our roles in the church—both locally and abroad. That's why we've organized our church the way we have—

to help each person find his or her place of service within the body of Christ. Let's take a few moments to look at the organization of our local body of believers.

BIBLE APPLICATION:
The Organization of the Organism

If you've asked a member of the pastoral staff to talk to your class about the organization of your local church, invite him or her to give that presentation now. Or give the presentation yourself. Be sure to cover topics like the role of the pastor, the roles of the staff members, information about cell groups, membership information, and any other information relevant to the particular organization of your local church.

After the presentation, allow time for participants to ask any questions they may have about the organization or ministry of your church.

TAKING ACTION:
Finding Your Place

Say:

> We can see that the church is not a building where people go but God's people in community doing what he has called us to do. We can know Christ through worship, study, prayer, submission, and obedience. We can make him known to others through loving, teaching, serving, and sharing our faith. The church is a living organism that brings change to the people in the world.
>
> There is a place reserved for you within this organism called the body of Christ. Each of us is called to a specific

purpose within the world and the body of Christ. It's important that we each discover God's unique call on our lives.

Give each person an index card. Then say:

This week think and pray about what God's call might be for you within the body of Christ. Where do you think God wants you to serve others within his body? Sometime this week write your thoughts about this important issue on your index card. Then bring the card with you to our next session. Also, please bring a personal cassette player to class next week for our class activity.

Close with prayer, then dismiss the class.

What and Why?

Section 1:
What is the Church?

Study the following Scriptures to find an answer to this question:

Ephesians 1:22-23	1 Corinthians 12:27
Revelation 19:7	Revelation 21:2
Ephesians 2:19	Ephesians 4:3-6
Romans 12:5	1 Corinthians 12:12, 25
Acts 2:46	2 Corinthians 6:18

Section 2:
Why is the Church here?

Study the following Scriptures to find an answer to this question:

John 13:34-35	Ephesians 3:20-21
2 Timothy 4:2	Galatians 6:10
2 Corinthians 4:5	1 Corinthians 10:31
Ephesians 2:10	Ephesians 4:11-12

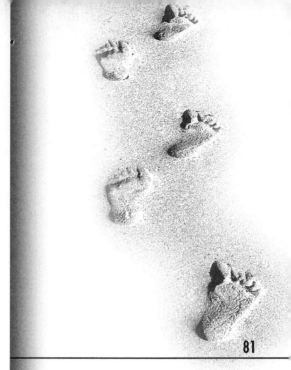

Knowing God's Call

SESSION 11

BEFORE THE SESSION

Telephone each participant, and ask him or her to bring a personal cassette player with fresh batteries to the next session. Also remind participants to bring the "index card" homework you assigned to them in the last session.

Using a cassette recorder, make a recording of the "Knowing God's Call" script (pp. 85-88). Then use a cassette-to-cassette recorder to make one duplicate of the cassette for each participant in the class. (Many churches have high-speed cassette duplication machines that you can use for this purpose.)

In the meeting room, create four stations for participants to visit. To create a station, form a circle of six chairs. In the center of the circle, lay down a crumpled-up, solid-colored sheet, then place several candles on top of the sheet. Make sure the candles have protective bases to catch melting wax. In the center of Station 1, place a small cross or a picture of a cross. In the center of Station 2, place a sheet of paper with the word "Listen" written on it. In the center of Station 3, place a sheet of paper with the following questions written on it:

- Is it Scriptural?
- Does it glorify Christ?
- Is it my passion?
- Is it consistent with my gifts and talents?

SUPPLIES NEEDED:

- Bibles
- paper
- pens
- extra personal cassette players
- cassette recording of the "Knowing God's Call" script (pp. 85-88) for each person
- extra batteries
- solid-colored sheet
- candles
- matches
- CD player
- background music
- cross (or picture of a cross)
- markers

• Does it meet a need?

In the center of Station 4, place a sheet of paper with the word "Trust" written on it.

In one corner of the room, set up a CD player to play soft, instrumental music. Set the music to play continuously. Shortly before participants arrive, start the music, light the candles, and, if possible, dim the lights in the room.

OPENER:
Homework Review

As participants arrive, direct them to an alternate room for this opening activity. If no room is available, you might be able to do this outside or in a foyer or hallway. Don't allow students to enter the primary meeting room until they are ready to begin the journey. You might provide coffee and light refreshments to encourage interaction while you wait for all to arrive.

Once everyone has arrived, ask volunteers to share what they wrote on their index cards about God's call on their lives. After a few people have shared, say:

Today's session is going to be very different. To discover God's call on our lives, we have to take time to look inward and ask ourselves some meaningful questions about our passions and our desires, as well as our talents and abilities. In this session, each of you is going to go on a private inward journey. Our regular meeting room has been transformed into a journey room. In a moment, I'll ask six of you to begin that journey. But first we'll need to make sure everyone has all the supplies you will need for this experience.

BIBLE EXPLORATION:

Entering the Journey Room

Make sure each person has a Bible, a working personal cassette player, and a cassette copy of the "Knowing God's Call" script, which you made before class. Give each person two sheets of paper and a pen. Have participants fold their papers together to form a four-page booklet. Tell them that they will use this booklet to record their thoughts and decisions as they go through their journey.

Select six people to begin the journey. Instruct them not to speak to one another once they enter the journey room. When their journey is complete, have them return to the alternate room to discuss their experience.

About seven minutes after sending the first group into the journey room, send another group of six into the journey room. Encourage individuals to take their time and to respect the privacy of other participants.

Have those who are waiting to enter the journey room form groups of six or fewer and read together the following Scripture passages. These same verses will be addressed once they enter the journey room:

Psalm 139:15-16	Psalm 40:8
Romans 12:1	Jeremiah 29:11
Psalm 46:10	Deuteronomy 30:20
1 Corinthians 1:9	Deuteronomy 7:9
Psalm 22:5	

BIBLE APPLICATION:

Discoveries From the Journey

As each group returns to the alternate meeting room, invite participants to talk about their experience with one another. Encourage them to discuss the following questions. You might want to write them on a chalkboard or newsprint for the groups' convenience in discussion.

• **What did you think of the journey you just took?**

- **What did you learn about yourself?**
- **What did you learn about discovering God's call on your life?**
- **What's one way you think God has called you to serve?**

TAKING ACTION:
Heeding the Greater Call

After each group's discussion time, encourage them to close by praying for one another, asking God to reveal his call on each of their lives.

As each group leaves, say:

Remember that there are some things all Christians are called to do—such as love one another, share your faith, and pursue a Christ-like lifestyle. Even if you don't yet know what specific call God has placed on your life, you can begin to serve him this week by doing these things.

Knowing God's Call

Record the following script onto a cassette tape. Pay attention to the bracketed instructions built into the script [like this]. Do not read aloud the instructions in brackets. Those instructions are for you alone.
Here is the script:

As you enter the journey room, move to the station that has a cross at its center. Sit down, and open your Bible to Psalm 139:15-16. Silently read what you find there. *[Pause for eight seconds.]*

Psalm 139 clearly assures us that there is a plan for each one of us that is specifically designed by God and prepared for us before time began. This is our call from him. Each of us in our Christian walk must answer the questions, "What is my call?" and "How do I personally carry out the ministry of Jesus?" To proceed with this quest, we must follow a plan to discover what God has created us to do. This journey will take you through the steps of that plan. *[Pause for five seconds.]*

The first step in discovering God's call on your life is to surrender yourself to God. Take a moment to read Psalm 40:8. *[Pause for fifteen seconds.]*

Is your desire to do God's will? Have you fully surrendered yourself to the Lord? Look at the cross in the center of the circle. What areas of your life are you still holding back from the cross? Look in the book of Romans, and read what it says in chapter 12, verse 1. *[Pause for fifteen seconds.]*

We must surrender everything to the cross of Christ. Surrender is not easy for any of us. We are taught to be independent, self-sufficient, make-your-own-decision kind of people. But to allow Jesus to be our Lord, we must surrender ourselves to him, giving him permission to carry out his plan through us. *[Pause for five seconds.]*

On one page of your booklet, write down any areas of your life that you need to surrender to God. *[Pause for thirty seconds.]*

When your list is complete, tear out the page on which you have written. Crumple it up, and lay it at the foot of the cross in the center of your circle. As you do this, consciously surrender to God each of the items you listed on your paper. *[Pause for twenty seconds.]*

When you have finished, stop the tape and move to the next station on your journey. It is the station with the word "Listen" in the center. *[Pause for thirty seconds.]*

Once you are seated at the next station, look up and read these three verses: Jeremiah 29:11 *[pause for twenty seconds]*; Psalm 46:10 *[pause for twenty seconds]*; and Deuteronomy 30:20 *[pause for twenty seconds]*. Through the Word God has told us that God has a plan for each of us. God will tell us what that plan is and guide us step by step if we take time to listen. Even though God is loving and just, we may be fearful of what we will hear or what God may ask us to do. This fear is unnecessary. God loves us, and God's will for our lives is born out of that love. We must lay aside our reservations and listen. Only by listening can we discern God's call for our lives.

Take some time now in silence, and listen to God. As you listen, write in your booklet anything you hear the Holy Spirit saying to you. For the next few minutes, turn off the tape, and listen in silence. When you are ready, move to the next station—the one with a list of questions in the center. Once you're seated at the next station, turn the tape back on. *[Pause for ten seconds.]*

Once you believe you've heard from God, the next step is to test what you've heard. Not everything we think we hear really comes from God. There are many other voices within us competing for attention. Our own desires, our fears, and the voice of the enemy all battle for dominance in our attempts to hear God in our spirits. *[Pause for five seconds.]*

In the center of the circle, you'll see a series of questions. These are some of the questions you must ask yourself to determine whether the call you hear is really from God or from some other source. If you cannot answer "yes" to all of these questions, then you may need to rethink whether the call you have heard is really from God. *[Pause for five seconds.]*

The first question is, "Is it Scriptural?" Is the call you are considering consistent with the commands and principles of God's Word? God will never call you to do anything that goes against what is taught in Scripture. In your booklet, write your answer to this first question. *[Pause for twenty seconds.]*

The second question is, "Does it glorify Christ?" The purpose of following God's call is not to glorify or call attention to us, but to point others to Jesus and life in him. Anything glorifying a person above God or dishonoring Christ is not of God. In your booklet, write your answer to this second question. *[Pause for twenty seconds.]*

The third question is, "Is it my passion?" God created each of us to be unique. Each of us has different things that bring us joy. God's plan for us is designed to fit the way he made us. As a result, we often have a strong desire to serve in a way that fits with the deepest desires of our hearts. In your booklet, write your answer to this third question. *[Pause for twenty seconds.]*

The fourth question is, "Is it consistent with my gifts and talents?" If we are searching for the way God will use us in his plan, it only makes sense that his plan would match up with and use the spiritual gifts and talents he has given us. What talents and gifts has God given you? Do these match up with the call you are considering? In your booklet, write your answer to this fourth question. *[Pause for twenty seconds.]*

The final question is, "Does it meet a need?" As you look around your community, where you live, can you see how this call can genuinely help other people? God does not call us to do things that are purely self-focused. Anything he calls us to do has the ultimate goal of serving others, meeting their needs, and helping them to know God. In your booklet, write your answer to this fifth and final question. *[Pause for twenty seconds.]*

When you are ready, move to the final station—the one with the word "Trust" in the center. *[Pause for twenty seconds.]*

Following God can seem risky because we give up control over our own destinies. Where will God take us? What will God call us to do? Will God protect us and keep us from making mistakes? As you ponder these questions, take a moment to read the following three Scriptures: Deuteronomy 7:9 *[pause for twenty seconds]*; 1 Corinthians 1:9 *[pause for twenty seconds]*; and Psalm 22:5. *[Pause for twenty seconds.]*

God is not safe in the human sense of the word. The Bible makes it clear that he can and will allow his children to make mistakes and to suffer for his sake. But God is good. And that is why we can trust him, wherever he leads. When we step out in faith, God will not disappoint us. We can depend on God to be faithful in keeping his promises.

In your booklet, write a brief prayer to God. Tell him how you feel about the call he has placed on your life. Tell him how you feel about letting go of your own plans in favor of his plans for you. Ask him to strengthen your faith so that you can follow his will boldly with all your heart, as you ought to. Thank him for choosing you and for the unique call he has placed on your life.

Turn off the tape, then write your prayer. When you have finished, you may return to the other room where your leader is waiting.

Where Will I Serve?

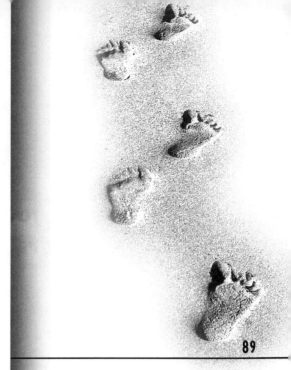

SESSION 12

BEFORE THE SESSION

Prepare a table full of treats and drinks for the participants to enjoy at the end of this session. When it is ready, cover the table with a sheet or something similar to keep participants from knowing what it is.

OPENER:
Dumb Excuses

Have participants form pairs and tell their partners the dumbest excuse they have ever used to avoid doing something they didn't want to do. After a few minutes, call everyone together, and have each person share with the class what his or her partner said.

Once everyone has shared, say:

We all use silly excuses to get out of doing things we don't want to do. Sometimes we even use excuses to avoid things we really do want to do but are afraid to try. We may be afraid to fail (or succeed), or perhaps we're afraid we will make the wrong choice. That's how it often is for Christians when they first step out to serve in the church. They may really want to do it deep down, but they are afraid of

SUPPLIES NEEDED:

- Bibles
- "Finding Your Place" handouts (pp. 93-94)
- pens
- newsprint
- tape
- markers
- treats
- drinks and other supplies for a celebration

doing something wrong—so they make excuses.

If you're like that, don't worry. You're in good company. Even the great and noble Moses made excuses when God called him at the burning bush. Let's look at some of the excuses he made. I suspect that at least some of them will look familiar.

BIBLE EXPLORATION:

Excuses, Excuses

Have a volunteer read Exodus 3:1-10 aloud. Then say:

This was Moses' call from God. Delivering Israel from Egypt was exactly what Moses had been made to do. His personality, his gifts, his upbringing, and his experience all made him the perfect man for the job. But Moses was afraid. And he made excuses.

Assign each person one of the following Scriptures: Exodus 3:11; Exodus 3:13; Exodus 4:1; Exodus 4:10; and Exodus 4:13. It's OK if more than one person is assigned the same Scripture.

Say:

One of Moses' excuses is contained in each of the Scriptures I've assigned. Your task is to read your assigned Scripture, find the excuse Moses used, and then come up with a modern equivalent excuse that Christians might use today. If you need help, feel free to work together with someone else who has been assigned the same Scripture.

While participants are working, tape a large sheet of newsprint to the wall, and divide it into five sections. In each section, write one the following references: Exodus 3:11; Exodus 3:13; Exodus 4:1; Exodus 4:10; and Exodus 4:13. When participants are ready, go through the list of Scriptures you assigned, and ask participants to tell you what they discovered. Record participants' observations on the newsprint in the appropriate section.

When the list is complete, have participants turn to a partner to answer these questions:

- Have you ever used one of these excuses to avoid doing something you know God wanted you to do? Explain.
- Why are we tempted to make excuses instead of serving God?
- How can we fight the impulse to make excuses when God calls us to serve him in some specific way?

After the discussion, call everyone together and say:

Last week we walked through the steps involved in discovering the call God has placed upon each one of us. Today we'll go one step further to come to an understanding of where to use that call within the church and our local community. To do that, we'll need to look at three areas: our passions, our spiritual gifts, and our personality style. Let's walk through these three areas together so we can each discover where we should serve in the local church and community.

BIBLE APPLICATION:
Finding Your Place

Have participants form groups of four or fewer, and give each person a pen and a copy of the "Finding Your Place" handout (pp. 93-94). Have groups work through the handout together. Encourage group members to help one another answer the questions and explore the issues raised by the handout. As groups work, walk around the room and offer to help any individual or group who is having trouble identifying his or her passions, gifts, or personality style.

When groups have finished, call everyone together, and ask several volunteers to share what they discovered about themselves or about other members of their group. Then say:

Everything we have talked about in the last twelve sessions can be summed up in the word *discipleship*. We have discussed God's expectations of each one of us. It's now up to you to take this information and allow it to transform your lives.

Tell participants to keep their handouts as an encouragement to follow through on their desire to serve God and his people in the local church and community.

EVALUATION AND CELEBRATION:
Look How Far We've Come!

Remove the sheet that is covering the table full of treats and drinks. Say:

> **We are so glad that you have been a part of this class. Now it's time to celebrate how far we've come together and to reflect on what we've learned about God, ourselves, and one another.**

Invite participants to enjoy the treats and drinks you have prepared. As they mingle, ask them to discuss with one another each of the following questions (you may want to write these questions on a sheet of newsprint where everyone can see them):

- **What has been especially meaningful to you in the past twelve weeks?**
- **What lessons have you taken to heart and already implemented in your life?**
- **What is the next step in your discipleship process?**
- **How can we improve this class to serve you better?**

As participants discuss these questions, walk around the room and listen in on their responses. Write down some of the comments you hear so that you can use them to improve the class the next time around.

After participants have had their fill of treats and drinks, dismiss the class with prayer, thanking God for each of the participants by name.

92

Finding Your Place

There are at least three things you need to know about yourself in order to find your place in the local church and community:

What are my passions?

What are my spiritual gifts?

What is my personality style?

Work together with your group to find your personal answer to each of these important questions. Use this handout as a guide.

1. What are my passions?—To help discover your passions, discuss these questions with your group:

- If you had no restrictions on your time or money, what types of people or special causes would you like to help?

- People have an inward desire to leave a legacy, to make a difference in the lives of others. What group of people or special cause would you like to serve in order to make a difference?

- If we were to interview your spouse or closest friend, what would they say you are passionate about?

2. What are my spiritual gifts?—A few weeks ago, you identified one or more spiritual gifts. Tell your group which gifts those are and why you think God has given them to you. Encourage those group members who know you well to tell you what spiritual gifts they think God has given you.

Here is a list of the spiritual gifts you studied, for your convenience:

- Exhortation (encouragement)
- Giving
- Leadership
- Serving
- Wisdom
- Knowledge

- Helps
- Miracles
- Administration
- Apostleship
- Teaching
- Prophecy
- Mercy

- Faith
- Healing
- Discernment of spirits
- Speaking in tongues
- Interpretation of tongues
- Pastoring (shepherding)
- Evangelism

3. What is my personality style?—To determine your style, look at the four boxes below.

QUADRANT 1:	QUADRANT 2:
People	Task
QUADRANT 3:	QUADRANT 4:
Lead, Organize, Plan	Behind the Scenes

Select your preference from the first row—People or Task. By that we mean, do you prefer to work with people, or do you prefer to work on a task without having to interact with people very much?

Next, select your preference from the second row—Lead, Organize, Plan or Behind the Scenes. By that we mean, do you prefer doing things that require you to lead, plan, and organize events or people, or do you prefer to work in a supporting role behind the scenes?

Now that you've selected your preferences, you can determine your personality style. For example,

Quadrants 1, 3—You like to lead groups of people and enjoy organizing and planning group activities.

Quadrants 2, 3—You like to lead in the planning and organizing of systems or programs to facilitate ministry.

Quadrants 1, 4—You like to serve with a group of people to support ministry events and activities.

Quadrants 2, 4—You like to serve on projects that require minimal interaction with people to support ministry events and activities.

The final step in the process involves pulling it all together—your passions, your gifts, and your personality style. Is there a type of service in which all of these areas intersect? Brainstorm with your group a list of ways of serving your church and community that bring together all three of these important areas. Write your ideas here:

94

Group Publishing, Inc.
Attention: Product Development
P.O. Box 481
Loveland, CO 80539
Fax: (970) 679-4370

Evaluation for
A Follower's Life

Please help Group Publishing, Inc. continue to provide innovative and useful resources for ministry. Please take a moment to fill out this evaluation and mail or fax it to us. Thanks!

● ● ●

1. As a whole, this book has been (circle one)

not very helpful   very helpful

1   2   3   4   5   6   7   8   9   10

2. The best things about this book:

3. Ways this book could be improved:

4. Things I will change because of this book:

5. Other books I'd like to see Group publish in the future:

6. Would you be interested in field-testing future Group products and giving us your feedback? If so, please fill in the information below:

Name _____

Church Name _____

Denomination _____ Church Size _____

Church Address _____

City _____ State _____ ZIP _____

Church Phone _____

E-mail _____

Never Settle for "Church as Usual" Again!

AN UNSTOPPABLE FORCE: DARING TO BECOME THE CHURCH GOD HAD IN MIND

Erwin Raphael McManus

"I love this book because Erwin loves the church. He understands what ministry is really like. So read it and learn. Read it with an open mind. The moment you think you've got the ministry all figured out, you're finished—in ministry and life. Growing churches require growing leaders. This book will help you along the way." —Rick Warren
Lead Pastor, Saddleback Church
Author, The Purpose Driven Church

This book will guide you through specific changes in culture that call for immediate change in the church. You'll get practical ways for your church to find its unique voice and identity to express Christ's love and faith to those around you.

ISBN 0-7644-2306-1   HARDCOVER

LOST IN AMERICA: HOW YOU AND YOUR CHURCH CAN IMPACT THE WORLD NEXT DOOR

Tom Clegg and Warren Bird

"Lost in America will help you identify fresh ways to relate the timeless message of Christ to searching people in your life today." —Franklin Graham
CEO, Billy Graham Evangelistic Association

Gain a fresh understanding of the spiritual needs of those outside the church and a compelling challenge to reach out to those without Christ. Lost in America will challenge the way you think about the spiritual climate in the United States and reveal the power that genuine friendship and love have to reach the spiritually hungry.

ISBN 0-7644-2257-X   HARDCOVER

AQUACHURCH: ESSENTIAL LEADERSHIP ARTS FOR PILOTING YOUR CHURCH IN TODAY'S FLUID CULTURE

Leonard Sweet

Discover the leadership arts that are essential in today's ever-changing culture. The author provides thought-provoking yet practical skills that will elevate the scope of ministry from mere survival of daily challenges to thriving in today's culture! Rather than provide new maps that will soon be obsolete, this book illustrates the need to become an "AquaChurch" in order to effectively minister in a fluid, postmodern culture.

ISBN 0-7644-2151-4   HARDCOVER

THE DIRT ON LEARNING

Thom & Joani Schultz

This thought-provoking book explores what Jesus' parable of the sower says about effective teaching and learning. Readers will rethink the Christian education methods used in their churches and consider what really works. Use the video training kit to challenge and inspire your entire ministry team and set a practical course of action for Christian education methods that really work!

BOOK ONLY   ISBN 0-7644-2088-7
VIDEO TRAINING KIT   ISBN 0-7644-2152-2

Discover our full line of children's, youth, and adult ministry resources at your local Christian bookstore, or write: Group Publishing, P.O. Box 485, Loveland, CO 80539.
www.grouppublishing.com